ENERGISE
THE SECRETS OF MOTIVATION

Professor Robert West
Jamie West

Copyright © Robert West and Jamie West 2019

The rights of Robert West and Jamie West to be identified as the authors of this work have been asserted in accordance with the Copyright, Designs and Patents Act 1988.

This edition first published in Great Britain in 2019 by Silverback Publishing.

All rights reserved. Apart from any use permitted under UK copyright law, this publication may only be reproduced, stored or transmitted, in any form, or by any means, with prior permission in writing of the publishers or, in the case of reprographic production, in accordance with the terms of licences issued by the Copyright Licensing Agency.

ISBN: 978-1-912141-13-5

Every effort has been made to fulfil requirements with regard to reproducing copyright material. The authors and publishers will be glad to rectify any omissions at the earliest opportunity.

www.silverbackpublishing.org

Contents

About This Book	4
1. What's My Motivation?	6
2. Who Is This Book For?	16
3. Does Any Of This Actually Work?	22
4. A 'Systems' Approach	28
5. Praise & Blame	36
6. Intrinsic & Extrinsic Motivation	42
7. Identity & The Unstable Mind	50
8. The 3Ts: Tension, Triggers, And Treatment	56
9. Creating Tension: Persuasion	64
10. Tricks Of Persuasion	76
11. Incentives	84
12. Coercion & Punishment	92
13. Conclusion: Wrapping Up	102
Glossary	110
Acknowledgements	116
About The Authors	118

About This Book

Energise developed out of summer workshops run by University College London's *Centre for Behaviour Change* which is attended by a diverse range of people including policymakers, business leaders, and researchers. The workshops are designed to offer a deeper understanding of human motivation, leading to practical applications.

I wrote this book with my son, Jamie, over the course of many conversations at an Italian café, near where I live, in North London. Our aim was to make the information easier to digest and allow for the kinds of problems that actually come up in daily life. Jamie is a freelance writer and performer, so the discussions on self-motivation were particularly pertinent for him!

Motivation is obviously a vast subject, and we can't cover everything in this slim volume. We've chosen to focus, instead, on exploring some simple yet game-changing principles. When applied, we believe they will dramatically increase your chances of successfully changing behaviour – both your own and other people's.

Robert West

1. What's My Motivation?

Jamie Go on, then – what *is* motivation?

Robert Good question. Let's start with what you think it is and we can work from there.

Jamie Well, I think of motivation when I see news stories about . . . husbands who've murdered their families or arms dealers selling weapons to despotic regimes.

Robert Cheery stuff!

Jamie The question I always ask is: what was their motivation? Was it money, jealousy, insanity? Or, I think of actors, head in hands, crying out, 'What's my motivation?!' I suppose motivation seems to lie at the heart of everything we do. It guides all of our behaviour.

Robert That's a very good start. I see motivation as a useful *construct* which helps us to understand why people do things and to predict behaviour. Also, if you can understand motivation well enough, you can influence behaviour both on a personal and collective scale.

Jamie That sounds promising . . . so motivation is . . . ?

Robert In everyday life, we tend to use the word 'motivation' in the context of getting someone to perform a certain behaviour – for example, how do I motivate my child to stop watching TV and do their homework? But motivation isn't the only factor that influences our behaviour. For that reason, first, we need to step back to look at the larger picture.

Jamie Okay.

Robert Motivation is one of *three* key things that need to be in place for a behaviour to occur. The first is *opportunity*. For example, if you want to become a guitarist, you need to have access to a guitar.

Jamie That's certainly true. What's the second?

Robert The second is *capability*. In other words, what you're physically and psychologically able to do. Playing the guitar requires skill and, no matter how many guitars you have, if you don't practise, you won't learn how to do it. Capability doesn't just involve skill, though. It also involves knowledge, understanding, self-control, and many other things.

Jamie I'm with you.

Robert So, capability and opportunity set the stage for the things you might potentially do. The third thing is *motivation*. Given all the things you could do, motivation determines what you actually do and how you do it.

Jamie That means that even though I have a guitar nearby, and am a capable guitarist, I still might decide to do something else – like eat an iced-ring donut, for example.

Robert That's right. We call this basic model of behaviour the *COM-B Model*. The three influences – *Capability (C)*, *Opportunity (O)*, and *Motivation (M)* – all feed into *Behaviour (B)*. It sounds technical, but it's actually quite straightforward.

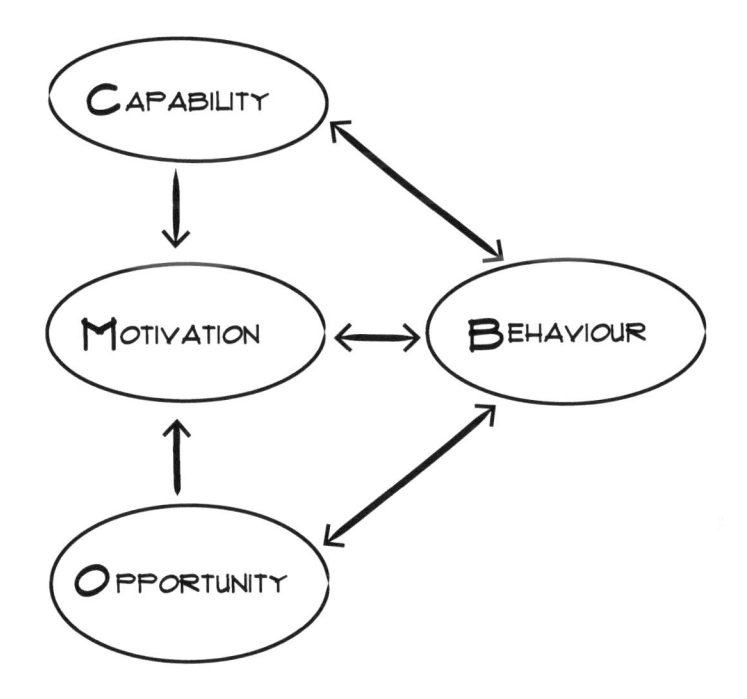

Robert In psychology textbooks, you will often see motivation defined as mental processes that energise and direct behaviour. This captures the fact that motivation doesn't just give us direction: it energises us to do things or not do things.

Jamie *Not* do things?

Robert Yes, motivation is critical to restraint. There's a famous case about a man called Phineas P. Gage, a 19th century railway construction foreman. One day, he was packing a charge of dynamite into a rock when the charge exploded too early, and a three-foot-long, one-inch-wide rod rocketed through Gage's face and skull up into the sky.

Jamie Wow.

Robert Amazingly, he survived the accident but he was a very different man after that. His speech, memory, and intelligence seemed okay, but his previous personality as a quiet, conventional man disappeared. He became so rude and irresponsible he couldn't hold down a job – at least for a time. He was constantly making plans then abandoning them immediately. He didn't follow through with anything. This drastic change was explained by the fact that the rod had damaged the part of his brain, his frontal lobes, needed to exercise self-restraint. His reckless behaviour consisted of things he had previously managed to keep under control. When the self-control went, there was nothing to stop his momentary desires and impulses from having free rein.

Jamie That's incredible. So, restraint – *not* doing things – is actually a very important part of motivation! If I started behaving without restraint I would very quickly lose my job, my girlfriend . . . Pretty much everything.

Robert Yes. Very often, those of us who work in the public health sector are trying to discourage harmful behaviours as much as encourage healthy ones.

Jamie Okay. Let's go back to motivation: are we consciously aware of what motivates us?

Robert Sometimes. When we talk about motivation, it involves terms like, 'I want this' or 'I need to this'. But it also includes things that don't enter into our conscious awareness. After all, much of our time is spent responding automatically with no thought at all.

Jamie So, motivation includes conscious and unconscious processes?

Robert Absolutely. All motivated behaviour involves unconscious processes. Breathing is a nice illustration of this.

Jamie Breathing involves our motivational system?

Robert Of course! We think of breathing as automatic, and most of the time it is. But not always. Let's do an experiment. I want you to take a deep breath and hold it for as long as you can.

Jamie What?

Robert Come on. Just do it.

Jamie Fine.

[10 seconds later]

Robert Seriously? 10 seconds?

Jamie I got bored.

Robert And you decided to breathe again?

Jamie Yes.

Robert Now, before I asked you to hold your breath, you probably weren't thinking about your breathing at all, were you?

Jamie No. I was thinking about that donut I mentioned earlier.

Robert Breathing is an instinctive behaviour: we do it without thinking. However, when I asked you to hold your breath, you were able to bring it under conscious control. But, at some point, you let go and started to breathe again.

Jamie Because I didn't feel like holding my breath anymore?

Robert The motivation for you to hold your breath was me asking you to do it. And you agreed to play along – though not very co-operatively. Now, I want you to hold your breath again, and really try to hold it for *as long as you can*.

Jamie I'll give it another shot.

[55 seconds later]

Robert Better. How was that?

Jamie I held it for as long as I could, but then I had to breathe.

Robert Interesting you say that. You reached a physiological point of needing oxygen?

Jamie I think so...

Robert Well, I can assure you that you were nowhere near the point at which, if you'd continued to hold your breath, you'd have suffered permanent tissue damage. Free divers – people who submerge themselves with no breathing equipment for as long as possible – train themselves to get to a point where they could actually suffer tissue damage. But most of us, including myself, and obviously you, give up long before then.

Jamie I didn't actually need to breathe?

Robert Your *urge* to breathe overwhelmed your *resolve* not to breathe.

Jamie Huh.

Robert A colleague of mine, Professor Peter Hajek, who works at Queen Mary University, made an interesting discovery about this at his stop smoking clinic. One of the things they do at the beginning is to get people to take a carbon monoxide breath test. It's similar to an alcohol breath test. You hold your breath for a few moments then you breathe into what's called a carbon monoxide monitor.

Jamie I've done one. It measures the amount of carbon monoxide in your blood showing if you've smoked recently.

Robert Peter noticed that when patients came into the clinic for the first time, some of them were unable to hold their breath for even 10 seconds. What he observed was that these people seemed more likely to drop out of the course and go back to smoking. He formulated a very simple hypothesis that people who tend to give in easily to pressure in the face of a decision to do something else – in this case, the pressure to breathe – are more likely to go back to smoking when they try to stop.

Jamie And did that turn out to be true?

Robert Yes. He ran a formal study which supported his hypothesis.

Jamie So, if I was really struggling to hold my breath for longer than 10 seconds, that might be a sign that I have weaker willpower?

Robert I wouldn't use the word 'willpower', but that's the basic idea. The point is, in that little scenario, we have one of the key narratives of human motivation. There are two conflicting forces: (1) A resolve not to breathe (2) The urge to breathe. And this battle between resolve and urge lies at the heart of so many of the problems we face in society in relation to behaviour change.

Jamie I imagine we all struggle with these kinds of internal battles every day?

Robert Constantly.

Jamie So, to recap: motivation energises and directs us to do things and *not* do things. It involves conscious and unconscious processes. One of the common themes that plays out is the internal struggle between our *resolve* to act in a certain way and our *urge* to act in a different way.

Robert Yes. And once you realise this, you will do a better job of influencing other people's behaviour and understanding how other people are trying to influence you . . .

KEY POINTS

- Motivation energises and directs us to do things and *not* do things.

- Motivation involves conscious and unconscious processes.

- There is often an internal struggle between our *resolve* to act in a certain way and our *urge* to act in a different way.

- Motivation (M) is one of three key things that feed into Behaviour (B). The other two are Capability (C) and Opportunity (O). This is known as the *COM-B Model*.

2. Who Is This Book For?

Jamie So, who might benefit from this book?

Robert *Energise* is for people who want a better understanding of human nature and how to influence behaviour.

Jamie Whose behaviour?

Robert The principles of motivation are the same for everyone. So, while we're learning about how best to motivate ourselves, we'll also be learning about how to influence other people.

Jamie Which will be useful in personal and professional contexts.

Robert Yes. I want our readers to go away with a broader and deeper understanding than most people currently have. So, when they are faced with an issue or have to make a decision, they can stand back, reflect, then bring into play all the different factors relevant to what they're trying to achieve. For example, a common misconception is that knowledge alone is enough to motivate people to do things. The thinking goes: 'If only we could get people to understand the benefits of tackling climate change, people would be more motivated to do it'.

Jamie That's not true?

Robert Well, sometimes altering knowledge or beliefs does change behaviour. But very often it's not enough on its own, and, quite often, it isn't even necessary. We need to broaden our perspective to understand all the other influences on behaviour, like drives, emotions, and habits.

Jamie I suppose it seems obvious now you've pointed it out: there's more to motivation than changing knowledge or beliefs.

Robert Right. But some people push it too far and fall into the opposite misconception that runs something like: 'Beliefs don't matter. If you want to change behaviour, you should "nudge" people so their behaviour is influenced unconsciously'.

Jamie I read about a study where pictures of flies were etched into urinals to get men to aim more carefully! Sort of controlling their behaviour without them realising it. But you're saying that's not the whole story?

Robert Drives, emotions, instincts and habits are crucial to behaviour, but so are beliefs.

Jamie So, a big problem with experts in motivation, and the lay public, is a tendency to focus on just one part of motivation and fail to see the bigger picture.

Robert Yes. I think that it's possible to get a wider understanding of behaviour by looking at how the motivation system works as a whole and by questioning how the different parts interact with one another. This also helps diagnose problem areas and figure out exactly what needs to change.

Jamie Right. Are diagnostic tools especially important?

Robert They're crucial. For example, does the problem lie in someone making ineffective plans? Or are the plans fine, but they're not being implemented properly? Or perhaps the person can't control their impulses? And so on.

Jamie Working out where the problem lies helps us determine how to solve it.

Robert Precisely.

Jamie When I'm writing song lyrics and I'm struggling with a particular line, sometimes that line isn't the problem – it's the previous one or a line in a different verse. Over the years, I guess I've learned to sit with the problem and experiment with different diagnoses and solutions.

Robert That's a very good point. Habits are not just related to action – we also have habits of thoughts and emotions. And this means that as we move from being a baby through childhood and adulthood, we are repeating patterns of associations and thoughts. And these patterns become very deeply ingrained. It's like a river which over the years creates a valley, then a ravine, then a canyon. And that's fine for good habits, but less fine for bad ones.

Jamie So, unless we challenge unhelpful habits of thought, we're somewhat trapped.

Robert Yes. But even if we challenge them, we may revert to those habitual thoughts and behaviours – often when under stress. Indeed, for many of us, it's not a question of *if*, it's a question of *when*.

Jamie A bit of a sobering thought, no?

Robert Well, the key is to be prepared so that we're not surprised when it happens – we have the tools available to get back on track. This will put us in a position to decide what course of action to take from there.

Jamie Reverting to old habits isn't necessarily game over?

Robert What's done is done. Whether you're trying to change your own behaviour or someone else's, you need to develop a strong sense of where you're going. Stepping back to reflect on the process is generally a good idea.

Jamie I imagine if you're in some kind of leadership role that's especially important?

Robert Yes. And that doesn't mean you have to be a government minister or running a company. You might be in charge of a small team somewhere, teach, or have influence in a social capacity. It will still be an important part of your role to step back and analyse the situations in a professional way, often in a scientific way, so that you have a better chance of coming up with an effective course of action.

Jamie So, whether you're trying to push through a policy that affects thousands of people or choosing how to act in a personal relationship, motivation is going to be a crucial factor.

Robert Absolutely. And throughout the book, we'll be offering tools that are applicable to a wide variety of situations. The tools will help when things go off the rails or, perhaps, stop things going off the rails in the first place.

KEY POINTS

- *Energise* is useful for people who want a better understanding of human nature and how to influence behaviour.

- It's important to look at changing behaviour from a variety of angles. There is no single technique or strategy that works all the time.

- If you want to change a behaviour, it's vital that you first diagnose the problem correctly.

- Habits don't just relate to our actions: we form habitual patterns of thoughts and emotions too.

3. Does Any Of This Actually Work?

Jamie Before we go any further, I want to set some expectations. Is it actually possible to change the behaviour of others? I imagine a therapist sitting in would tell us to just focus on changing ourselves. Although, I suppose, that doesn't stop us from wanting to change other people.

Robert There's a good evolutionary reason for wanting to change other people. If we can change other people, they'll do what we want and our goals will align. We can get on with building our mud hut, hamlet, spacecraft, or Lego toy town. And we all have problems that need solving. How does a manager motivate a demoralised workforce? How does a parent get their child to stop throwing temper tantrums in the supermarket? Sometimes we're successful, but very often we're not. Most of the time, we have one tactic or tool and we keep using it whether or not it's effective. I want to increase our success rate in changing other people's behaviour by using a more evidence-based approach.

Jamie Bearing in mind that we won't be successful all of the time.

Robert Absolutely. As we build our understanding of motivation, we'll develop a clearer idea of how and when it's appropriate to intervene.

Jamie I can imagine all kinds of scenarios when intervening could end up being disastrous – particularly when dealing with large populations.

Robert Oh, yes. We'll talk about the power of advertising and marketing, amongst other things, later on. For now, it's enough to say that, obviously, some things can be changed and some things can't.

Jamie   There's no 'one-size-fits-all' solution.

Robert   That's right. An effective approach when looking at a motivational problem is to take into account the particular behaviour you want to change, the person or people you're targeting, and any relevant situational factors. A central aim of this book is to give readers a sense of the different tools available. That way, they can gain a better understanding of what their options are in a variety of situations.

Jamie   You said that we often only rely on using one method whether or not it works. So, we need to pay closer attention to whether something is working and, if it isn't, to be prepared to change what we're doing.

Robert   Exactly. When new evidence comes in, we need to be open to what this might mean for us. For example, people used to believe that stomach ulcers were mostly caused by stress. I remember a comedy writer saying that he developed his first stomach ulcer writing jokes for Bob Hope! But now we realise that stomach ulcers are mostly caused by bacteria.

Jamie   So, we can't blame Bob Hope anymore! But it's not always easy to be open to new information, is it? Our pride can really take a hit.

Robert   It's mentally less taxing to think of things as black-and-white or 'one-size-fits-all'. The reality is usually shades of grey.

Jamie   Cognitive Behavioural Therapy (CBT) categorises black-and-white thinking as a distorted way of thinking that can often lead to problems.

Robert And we're drawn to those types of thoughts like moths to a flame.

Jamie I recently watched a documentary about the actor Alec Guinness, probably most famous for playing Obi-Wan Kenobi in *Star Wars*. One of the people interviewed said that Guinness was never early and never late: he was always *exactly* on time. It really stuck with me. That kind of unfailing precision gave an extra dimension to his character. It defined him in a way.

Robert It's an interesting story, but, frankly, I doubt it. The implication, I think, is to do with power and control. Alec Guinness was able to control not just his own behaviour but that of external circumstances that might lead to a person being late.

Jamie As though he had some special *force*...

Robert (*laughs*) Which is tempting to believe, but think about it: what would it take and how possible would it be for Alec Guinness to have *always* been *precisely* on time? As we've been saying, the truth is usually more complicated and nuanced. We need to move away from myth-making and black-and-white thinking, and start focusing more on the reality of a situation.

Jamie I know you get frustrated by the lack of nuance in newspaper articles, particularly ones about e-cigarettes.

Robert Yes. I run a team of researchers who are trying to find the best ways to help people stop smoking – so I do know something about this topic. There are headlines describing studies that would lead you to think that e-cigarettes are just as dangerous as cigarettes. In fact, all the study has done is to show that e-cigarettes probably cause *some* harm to users – which is very different, but it doesn't make such a good story. Imagine the headline: 'E-cigarettes not totally safe but a lot safer than conventional cigarettes'.

Jamie Black-and-white statements have a huge amount of power. Grey sounds pretty boring.

Robert It lacks the punch, but it's often where we find the truth.

Jamie The other thing I want to quickly mention – for the perfectionist types, like me – is that the techniques in this book aren't necessary to use all the time. We don't want to be analysing everything in our lives, do we? Constantly trying to figure out what someone else is thinking and how to motivate them?

Robert That would be very tiring. The kinds of things we're talking about in this book relate to situations that matter.

Jamie Situations that aren't going to plan...

Robert And are worth the time and trouble to find a suitable strategy for dealing with them. In the everyday flow of behaviour, we just get on with doing stuff. And you don't have to be an expert in behaviour to make use of the principles we're describing in this book.

Jamie *I'm* certainly not an expert. But there are many times I've used the strategies we're discussing and achieved great results. Usually, it starts with me asking myself what I actually want to get out of a situation and working from there. But, I'm skipping ahead...

Robert That's right. All in good time.

KEY POINTS

- Sometimes we can change other people's behaviour; sometimes we can't. Learning about different motivation tools helps us to recognise what options are available to us and when they're most likely to be effective.

- An effective approach to solving a motivation problem will take into account the particular behaviour you want to change, the person or people you're targeting, and any relevant situational factors.

- Beware of 'black-and-white' thinking – the truth tends to be nuanced.

- Strategies should be based on evidence, and we should be prepared to change our opinions or strategies when new evidence comes in.

4. A 'Systems' Approach

Jamie How would you characterise your approach to understanding motivation?

Robert I use what experts in the field call a 'systems' approach. So, I don't start from the premise that motivation is all about beliefs, or drives, or environment, or feelings. I start from the premise that motivation is part of an interacting system which involves people and their environment.

Jamie And because the system has lots of things going on, you need to consider more than one angle.

Robert Right. The task is to map out what the influences are and how they interact with the different internal and external processes. This leads to a more precise and comprehensive analysis of what motivation is and how you can use motivation to influence behaviour.

Jamie And where have these ideas developed from?

Robert There are a large number of theories in the fields of behavioural science, psychology, sociology, anthropology, economics, and neuroscience. Many of them capture profound insights. Much of my work has been helping to bring these ideas into a unified picture.

Jamie Can you give me an example?

Robert Let's think about how our basic biological drives, such as hunger, interact with complex thought processes involving *identity* and, in the following scenario, social pressure.

Jamie Ah, okay...

Robert Here's the situation: you're in your local pub having a few drinks. You're trying to lose weight, but you're hungry. A friend opens a packet of crisps, lays them out on the table and says, 'Help yourself'. Now, your biological drive (hunger) is interacting with an environmental trigger (the offer of crisps) to generate an *urge*. However, your identity as someone trying to lose weight is generating a *resolve* to resist it. You inch towards the packet, but your partner raises an eyebrow and says, 'I thought you said you were on a diet?' Now, social pressure comes into the mix. You sit back. But while everyone else is chatting, the salty fried potatoes are there calling to you. Your partner goes to the loo. You grab a handful and scoff the lot down . . . Your diet can start tomorrow.

Jamie This is sounding eerily familiar!

Robert So, we have an interacting system involving the pub, your friend, your partner, your identity, hunger, crisps on the table, and, of course, time. A comprehensive approach to understanding what is going on here needs to capture all of these things and how they interact. Not an easy task – but not impossible either.

Jamie It's interesting that you use the word 'identity'. Why is this important in motivation?

Robert Let's take another example – say, you're somebody who loves mountain climbing, and you want to scale Mount Everest. Now, that's not a small mountain. If you try to climb it, you're putting your life at risk. Why are you doing it?

Jamie I don't know – I'm scared of heights!

Robert The climber George Mallory reportedly said the reason he did it was: 'Because it's there'.

Jamie That's pretty profound. I guess what's also contained in that phrase is: 'Because *I'm* here'.

Robert Identity can be so powerful it can overcome our most basic need to stay safe. I think for a lot of climbers, there's a drive to achieve something few others have achieved.

Jamie So, there are competing forces inside of us, but what controls them?

Robert Some people think in terms of a little person that sits inside our heads, a voice that controls or directs our behaviour.

Jamie The author Robert Wright talks about it as being like a CEO in our brains.

Robert Exactly. But, as he points out, that's an illusion. The reality is there's *no one thing* in control of our behaviour.

Jamie Are you sure?

Robert Well, what do you think is in charge of your behaviour?

Jamie I guess: *I* am.

Robert But as a Buddhist might say: 'Who is the "I" in that sentence?' The reason we think of our experience as a unified whole, with 'I' at the centre of it, is because we have no outside reference point. Imagine that your brain was suddenly switched off for 10 seconds then switched back on – what would that feel like to you?

Jamie Slightly odd?

Robert It wouldn't feel like anything unless you noticed something had changed in your surroundings. We've all had times where we've nodded off and not noticed it until someone has pointed it out to us. We think of our life as one coherent continuous experience – but it isn't.

Jamie So, our concept of ourselves, and I guess other people's selves, is somewhat of an illusion. But if that's true, and there are just different parts of our brain controlling us, then are we really responsible for our behaviour?

Robert Yes and no. Attributing responsibility for things is something that has evolved in order to control behaviour. Let's take an example: a child gets chosen to be the library monitor for their class. They're responsible for putting books back on the shelves. It's pretty clear that if the child is 'responsible', they will put the books away and the library will function well. The child will probably get praised for doing a good job. But if they're 'irresponsible', they'll put the books away incorrectly, or not at all, causing chaos. If they do well they're rewarded with praise, and if they're irresponsible they're blamed. The child knows this and so do their fellow pupils, and that contributes to everyone behaving 'responsibly'.

Jamie I don't know why you're looking at me like that – I was a very good library monitor!

Robert So you say. Anyway, responsibility allows the allocation of *praise* and *blame*, and these are social *rewards* and *punishments* which have developed in order to get us to want or need to do things – or *not* do things.

Jamie   As in the case of poor Phineas P. Gage.

Robert   Exactly. This may be hard to take for some people but if you want to be effective at changing behaviour, you have to look at praise and blame primarily as methods of social control, not ways of meting out justice. When you realise that, you can use them much more effectively to influence behaviour.

Jamie   We need to recognise that responsibility – just from the point of view of motivation – is something that is used socially to control behaviour.

Robert   And that's internalised through the process of socialisation so that we develop a sense of right or wrong. Society as a whole sets up moral values around things that are good and bad. At an individual level, people internalise things in different ways. So, if you're using praise and blame as tools to change someone's behaviour, you have to think about what matters to that person in terms of his or her core values. Otherwise, you're wasting your efforts . . . at best.

KEY POINTS

- Motivation is part of an interacting system which involves people and their environment.

- Identity is a crucial part of human motivation and can be harnessed to change behaviour in profound ways.

- There is no CEO sitting in our brains controlling what we do – there are always competing forces inside us trying to get us to do or *not* do things.

- Responsibility is a social construct used to control behaviour by allocating praise and blame to individuals and groups.

- If you use responsibility as a tool to change behaviour, think about what matters to the person you're trying to change – what are their core values?

5. Praise & Blame

Jamie Let's delve a bit more into *praise* and *blame*. I've heard you mention many times over the years that if we want people to stop behaving badly, we shouldn't rush into using *punishment*.

Robert Yes. When someone is doing something you don't want them to do, don't automatically punish them. It might feel like the natural thing to do, but very often it leads to a downward spiral. It's far better to stop and think about what's driving that behaviour and what's needed in order for that behaviour to change. That simple message can stop a lot of dysfunctional cycles.

Jamie I can definitely think of times in my life when I've reacted in the heat of the moment, and the situation just got worse and worse. But why does it feel natural to want to punish others when they've done something wrong?

Robert We're programmed to want people who do bad things to suffer! And it makes us feel good to punish what we see as bad behaviour. Even if the situation then gets worse as a result, we feel like we've expressed ourselves and 'got it off our chest', so to speak. But many times that's the worst possible way of changing someone's behaviour. If anything, they'll move further away from the behaviour we want.

Jamie And blame is a particular type of punishment?

Robert Blame is assigning moral responsibility to something that's judged to be bad. And when that blame is expressed in some way – it might be just a small facial expression – it's punishing.

Jamie I heard on the radio the other day that an NHS trust was considering whether to delay treatment for obese patients until they lost a certain amount of weight. And people were calling in and getting quite heated, blaming obese people for not having enough willpower to lose the weight.

Robert It's an idea that comes up quite a lot and is based on a failure to understand what is needed for weight control, which is a complex issue involving many interacting factors. The main point here is that blaming people might make *us* feel better, but it often doesn't help them to change their behaviour.

Jamie Does blaming people go back to this mistaken idea that we have a CEO sitting inside our heads controlling our behaviour? So that people who don't behave 'correctly' are simply not 'trying hard enough'?

Robert Exactly. To understand motivation, you have to realise that there are parts of our brain that create a sense of agency, order, and planning. Sometimes, those parts control our actions; much of the time, they don't. If you're trying to help someone recover from an addictive disorder, you're trying to strengthen the parts of the motivational system involved in forming and executing plans and weaken the parts of the system driving the maladaptive behaviour.

Jamie Is that something to do with strengthening the prefrontal cortex in our brains?

Robert The prefrontal cortex is very much involved in the formation and execution of plans. Drugs that disrupt the function of this part of the brain do seem to undermine an individual's capacity to develop and execute plans.

Jamie You often talk in your lectures about the seemingly simple idea that 'feeling good and feeling bad' lie at the heart of motivation.

Robert I'm glad you've been paying attention! That's right. And feeling good and feeling bad can stem from a vast range of different types of experience – from basic biological drives, such as hunger or thirst, all the way through to things like spirituality.

Jamie And is it the biological drives that dominate?

Robert It depends. Abraham Maslow proposed a hierarchy of needs which was interpreted as saying that biological drives tend to dominate. Although, as Maslow himself recognised, that's clearly not always the case. There are many circumstances in which what look like social, spiritual, or abstract values dominate.

Jamie Things that are to do with our *identity*.

Robert Like with the mountain climbers.

Jamie So, I guess our instinctive attraction towards using praise and blame to influence other people's behaviour is due to an intuitive understanding that feeling good and feeling bad lie at the heart of motivation.

Robert There's a certain irony in the fact that giving praise and blame arises out of the anticipation of feeling *good* by the person who's doing the praising or blaming!

Jamie I blame someone else because it makes me feel better not because it's necessarily going to change their behaviour?

Robert That's it in a nutshell.

Jamie But don't we kind of hate it? Being manipulated by praise and blame? I remember you trying to get me to do the washing up by overly praising me when I did it.

Robert You seemed to find it annoying.

Jamie It *was* annoying!

Robert *(laughs)* Bad example. But praise can be very effective. It expresses a positive moral judgment for something judged to be good. And, in general, the advice is: be generous with praise.

Jamie Don't get me wrong, I do like praise. And it usually does feel rewarding.

Robert Interestingly, we even find being praised by a computer rewarding. Think about completing an online course, or a video game. You get praised – and it feels good!

Jamie And that's just a piece of code.

Robert The only caveat I would mention is to be careful of becoming sycophantic – so, if you're praising someone of higher status than you, it may look like you're only praising them to curry favour.

Jamie How very perceptive of you, Professor...

Robert Which is not to say that flattery isn't effective! But just be aware of that possibility. Praise works especially well when it comes from a source of authority or someone you like.

Jamie It seems as though praise and blame are pretty fundamental tools.

Robert Yes. Although, it's vital to analyse *when* and *how* to use them. And, of course, there are many other tools we can use apart from praise and blame. As we better understand the motivational system, we can decide which tools are the most effective ones to influence any given behaviour. It sounds Machiavellian, but there are many tools we can use to shape behaviour where the people being targeted are not aware we're shaping their behaviour.

Jamie Going back to the idea of 'nudging' them.

Robert Right. That's why supermarkets put impulse purchase items, like chocolates, near the checkout. Or why some restaurants serve small Pinot Grigios in enormous wine glasses – though a large glass also enhances the bouquet I'm told! But it's important to note that there are many other options open to us apart from praise and blame. And, remember, don't rush to blame someone unless it's really necessary.

KEY POINTS

- Feeling good and feeling bad lie at the heart of motivation.

- Blame is assigning moral responsibility to something judged to be bad.

- When someone is behaving in a way you don't want, don't immediately punish them. Punishing often feels good to the *punisher*, but it's not necessarily effective in changing behaviour.

- Praise is expressing moral responsibility to something judged to be good.

- Be generous with praise.

- While praise and blame can lead to effective results, there are many other ways to change behaviour.

6. Intrinsic & Extrinsic Motivation

Jamie Okay, so we've established I hate washing up – and praise doesn't help. How else could you motivate me to do it?

Robert One route might be to pay you.

Jamie I'm listening...

Robert That would be tapping into something called *extrinsic motivation*. Essentially, this refers to wants and needs that are attached to a particular behaviour through some *reward* or *punishment* that has nothing to do with the behaviour per se.

Jamie That's quite a mouthful. You're saying, the only reason I'm doing the washing up is because I'm being paid to do it? It's got nothing to do with whether I enjoy washing up or not.

Robert Correct. And the opposite of extrinsic motivation is *intrinsic motivation*. That would be if you actually liked washing up or got a sense of satisfaction from it. Intrinsic motivation refers to wants and needs that relate to the behaviour itself.

Jamie So, if I found scrubbing plates fulfilling, no one would need to pay me to do it.

Robert Right. But, if they did, it might change your behaviour around washing up. You might end up only doing it for the money.

Jamie Michael Sandel, the political philosopher, calls it 'crowding out'. The financial incentive 'crowds out' the intrinsic motivation.

Robert And that's an important point if you're going to start using extrinsic motivators, like money, to get people to do things. There may be unintended adverse consequences. Let's take an important real-world example. GPs in the UK were expected, as part of their job, to advise people to stop smoking. But they didn't do it often enough. So a financial *incentive* was introduced: GPs were *paid* to advise people to stop smoking. However, researchers found that while GPs ticked a box saying they had provided advice, there had actually been no meaningful change in their behaviour. Worse still, it undermined their sense that this was a core part of their role.

Jamie So, you have to think carefully before paying people to do things.

Robert Which isn't to say money can't work incredibly well at motivating people to do a good job. If I wasn't being paid to do my job, I think I'd enjoy it a lot less, and I wouldn't do such a good job – or do it at all for that matter!

Jamie I used to play lots of free gigs as a musician, but, even though I found playing music rewarding, *not* getting paid eventually 'crowded out' my intrinsic motivation. It became less fun, the gigs were less rewarding, and eventually I stopped doing that kind of work.

Robert It's different for different people.

Jamie But I don't think any amount of money would make me truly enjoy an activity I wouldn't otherwise like. Isn't it better to be intrinsically motivated?

Robert Not necessarily. In many discussions around the subject, there is an implicit assumption that intrinsic is good and extrinsic is bad.

Jamie Money being the root of all evil.

Robert Actually, the King James Bible translation is: 'Love of money is the root of all evil' which makes a bit more sense. But a useful re-conceptualisation around extrinsic motivation is that it is *necessary*. In fact, there are certain things that no one will do unless they're extrinsically motivated. And it doesn't always mean paying someone – it could mean offering extra privileges or status.

Jamie Like VIP passes to a big music festival?

Robert Yes, that kind of thing.

Jamie I suppose thinking of extrinsic motivation as a bad thing could be related to the negative perceptions of neo-liberalism which, roughly speaking, is in favour of marketising almost everything. It can make people feel that everything is for sale, including values and beliefs.

Robert And, clearly, we have evidence that extrinsic motivators don't achieve our goals in particular areas – as with the GPs in my example. But neither does it mean that markets and money aren't motivating in other areas.

Jamie Hold on a moment. So, when we start to believe that everything should be extrinsically motivated, or indeed, intrinsically motivated, we're falling back into the trap of black-and-white thinking!

Robert As I've said before – it's not 'one-size-fits-all'.

Jamie And, crucially, we need to take a pragmatic approach. It doesn't matter if I *should* be intrinsically motivated to do something. The question is: what motivational tools are going to be effective for me in this situation?

Robert You got it. When you're trying to influence behaviour, think about what will realistically work, not about how you think the world *should* be.

Jamie I suppose intrinsic and extrinsic motivation can feed into each other. For example, you brought me up vegetarian, primarily for ethical reasons. It had nothing to do with whether I liked the taste of meat or not. But now, if I accidentally eat a piece of chicken, I spit it out and usually feel a bit queasy. So, even though I became a vegetarian for extrinsic reasons, I'm now intrinsically motivated to be a vegetarian because I don't like the taste of meat.

Robert You probably also get a sense of satisfaction from acting in accordance with your values, which is also an intrinsic motive.

Jamie It seems the lines between intrinsic and extrinsic motivation can get a bit fuzzy.

Robert Absolutely. There's a classic study on rats that highlights this.

Jamie Those poor rats.

Robert Imagine a hungry rat in a cage: if it presses a lever, a food hatch opens. The rat learns to press the lever and is rewarded by food. Now, imagine, after a period of time, the lever stops delivering food. What do you think happens?

Jamie The rat stops pressing the lever.

Robert Correct. Now, let's change the experiment slightly. In this new version, the rat still learns to press the lever, but, when the food hatch opens, something else happens as well: a light just above it briefly goes on. After some time, the food stops being delivered but the light continues to flash when the rat presses the lever. What do you think happens next?

Jamie I honestly don't know.

Robert The rat continues to press the lever – and for much longer than in the first experiment. The light has become rewarding in its own right just by being associated with the food. It has become what psychologists call a *'secondary reinforcer'*. The rat is pressing the lever to see the light! By the way, food is what we call a *'primary reinforcer'* – it is an innately programmed reward.

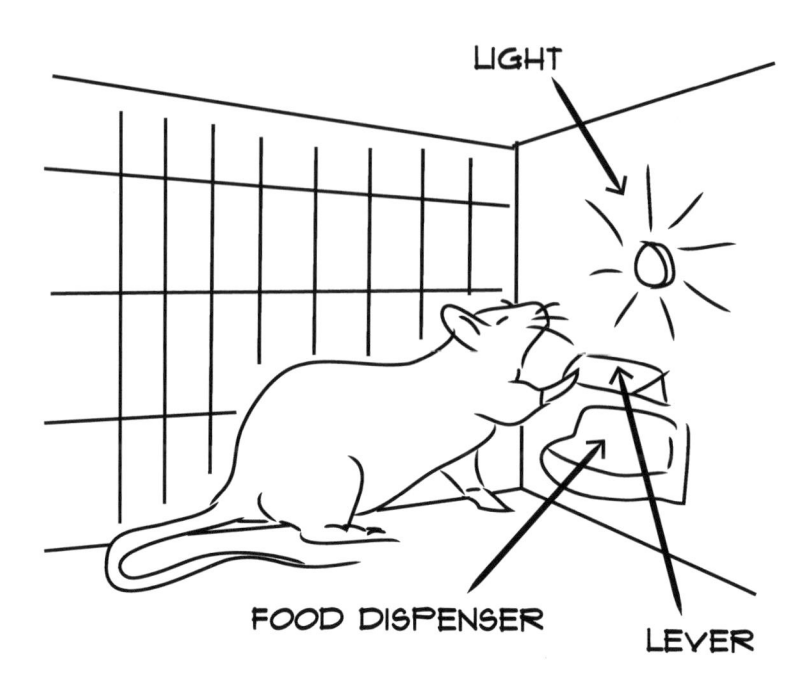

Jamie How does that relate to what we were talking about?

Robert Let me ask you this: is money an extrinsic or intrinsic reward?

Jamie Well, you can't eat it or do much with it apart from spend it, so I guess it must be an extrinsic reward.

Robert But it *feels* satisfying to have a nice big wad of notes in your hand! Money takes on a significance of its own like the light in the rat experiment. Acquiring it becomes rewarding in itself. We have a tendency to like things with good associations. And we can harness this tendency to influence behaviour.

Jamie Like apps that reward you with points when you do certain things.

Robert Yes. I get a kick out of hitting 10,000 steps because my Fitbit watch buzzes on my wrist – the buzz is strangely rewarding. Getting something to be intrinsically rewarding has a big advantage in that it doesn't need to be policed – extrinsic motivation does.

Jamie Margaret Atwood quotes an old Sufi proverb in the epigraph to her novel *A Handmaid's Tale*: 'In the desert there is no sign that says, Thou shalt not eat stones'.

Robert Exactly. Because no one wants to do it.

Jamie It sounds like there's a kind of happy middle point that uses both types of motivation. So, what insights does the intrinsic and extrinsic motivation distinction leave us with?

Robert If you want to get someone to do something, try to get them to *want* to do it for its own sake because they like it or find it satisfying. If you can't manage that, you can look to extrinsic motivation – you can bribe or reward them, threaten or punish them. But you'd better watch out for unintended consequences! We'll be looking more at the role of incentives and coercion later in the book.

KEY POINTS

- Extrinsic motivation relates to behaviour that is driven by external rewards or punishments, e.g. someone who is not interested in washing cars but will wash cars to earn money.

- Intrinsic motivation relates to behaviour that is driven by internal rewards or punishments, e.g. someone who washes their car because they enjoy washing their car.

- The definitions for intrinsic and extrinsic motivation can get a little fuzzy, but they're a useful starting point to help understand what motivates us.

- When you're trying to influence behaviour, focus on what will realistically work – not what you think *should* work.

- If you want to get someone to do something, try to get them to *want* to do it for its own sake because they like an aspect of it or find it satisfying.

- Introducing financial incentives for activities that are intrinsically rewarding can backfire, as it can change the relationship between the person and the activity – the financial incentive may 'crowd out' the intrinsic motivation.

7. Identity & The Unstable Mind

Jamie Earlier, we talked about identity as an important driver of behaviour. It seems to me that many people have a more fragile sense of identity these days. This seems to have developed alongside social media and globalisation – like there's a need for constant affirmation and validation from all around us. At the same time, we're also exposed to so many more different identities from across the world. Does this make it harder for us to build an individual sense of identity?

Robert Well, it's an interesting hypothesis – that modern life, through exposure to social media has led us to externalise our identities in a way that we didn't before. It's certainly possible. It's also possible that the channel through which we gain and sustain our identities has shifted.

Jamie So, the environment in which we form our identities has changed.

Robert As John Donne puts it: 'No man is an island'. We are fundamentally interconnected. If you live in a small social group without access to broader networks, that's what you'll care about and derive your identity from. Social media can broaden out these networks considerably. However, it's important to remember that, no matter what the environment, our identities are more fragile than we tend to think.

Jamie Why's that?

Robert Our minds are in a constant state of flux. They evolved to be like that because it allows us to learn and adapt very quickly. I like to use the term 'The Unstable

Mind' to refer to this, meaning that our minds are inherently unstable and require constant balancing input to stay on the straight and narrow.

Jamie I like that: 'balancing input'.

Robert It's like a modern 'fly-by-wire' jet aircraft that needs constant adjustment from computers to keep it on course. We need constant input from our social and physical environment to stop our thoughts and emotions spiralling out of control.

Jamie And social media provides us with opportunities for communication, approval, and to get reflections of ourselves.

Robert I think it's possible that none of this has changed the fundamental nature of identity. It may have just changed the expression of it and the way it's constructed.

Jamie So, our interaction with our environment and social groups – whether virtual or face-to-face – helps us to form our sense of self?

Robert Correct. One of the things that is very clear with people who get into serious difficulty with drugs and alcohol is that their identities are very often fractured. A positive strong sense of self is important for mental health. But people who get into trouble with drugs and alcohol very often don't have that for all kinds of reasons: early childhood experiences with abusive or neglectful parents, etc.

Jamie What does this strong sense of self do?

Robert It is the basis for exercising something very important: self-control.

Jamie Which is what, exactly?

Robert Self-control is the link between the part of your brain that forms plans and the part of your brain that feels urges to do other things.

Jamie Back to our resolve vs urge conflict!

Robert Precisely. Self-control mediates between planning and goals, on the one hand, and immediate wants and needs, on the other. And it can only really arise if you have a sense of self. You can only say, 'I intend to do this' if you have a sense of 'I', and that will only carry on if that sense of 'I' is something that is valued and has stability. So, a stable, positive self-identity is crucial for effective self-control.

Jamie And self-control is presumably necessary to set and reach long-term goals?

Robert That's right.

Jamie But doesn't this contradict your previous point that identities are fragile? And also the earlier argument about there being no CEO sitting in our heads, no 'I'?

Robert No. It is a strong *sense* of self that is the important thing. But anyone's identity can be undermined if they find themselves in a situation where all of their reference points have gone.

Jamie That makes me think of the Red Dwarf episode, 'Back To Reality'. The characters discover they've been living in a computer simulation and are actually not who they thought they were at all. Instead, they're quite horrible people and they come to hate themselves.

Robert I remember the episode – things quickly go from bad to worse! To make it even weirder, their 'discovery' was itself an illusion brought about by toxins produced by a giant squid...

Jamie Ah, I love science fiction! Can you imagine if – as we were talking – I saw pixels form on your face, then the whole world fell away, and I was left on a sort of Star Trek holodeck!

Robert Yes...

Jamie Everything I had previously thought about the world would dissolve in that instant!

Robert It certainly would. More down-to-earth examples would include a marriage breaking up or someone close to you dying.

Jamie So, identity – because it's based on receiving and reacting to reference points – is fundamentally unstable.

Robert And even a strong sense of self is fluid and subject to modification.

Jamie But even though our minds are inherently unstable, and our identities are fundamentally fragile, we still need to strive to develop a strong sense of ourselves?

Robert It sounds odd, but that's right – it's vital to feel a sense of personal agency.

Jamie The comedian Dave Chappelle said that being paid a lot for his Netflix specials gave him a false sense of security, but that a false sense of security was better than no sense of security!

Robert As Homer Simpson said: 'It's funny because it's true'.

KEY POINTS

- Our minds evolved to be in a constant state of flux – this allows us to learn and adapt quickly.

- 'The Unstable Mind' refers to the concept that our minds are inherently unstable and require constant balancing input to function well.

- A positive, strong *sense* of self is important for mental health. It also enables us to exert self-control.

8. The 3Ts: Tension, Triggers, And Treatment

Jamie You've said throughout our conversation that we need to adjust our approach to changing motivation based on the particular situation.

Robert Our approach has to be tailored to the behaviour we are trying to influence, the person, and the situation. And the tools we're discussing help to provide a framework to tackle problems.

Jamie And why do we need a framework?

Robert That's a very good question.

Jamie Don't sound so surprised!

Robert The thing is, we often rely on our intuition and common sense to solve problems, and that can be effective. In fact, as readers use the tools we're talking about in *Energise*, they'll find their intuition will begin to guide them better and better. That's because our intuitions are affected by our experience. But there are also many occasions when our intuitions and common sense point us in the wrong direction. When faced with problems regarding motivation, we rush to faulty diagnoses and faulty solutions. Then we feel over-confident in these solutions, which often don't succeed, and *then* we blame someone else.

Jamie *(laughs)* That sounds familiar.

Robert It's no great moral failing. It's just the way most of our brains work. That's why it's important to create a framework based on the different motivational tools available to us. We can then 'plot' our problem against this which will help us to make better diagnoses and choose more effective solutions.

Jamie Okay, I'm on board. What's next?

Robert We're going to start putting into practice what we've been discussing. Let's look again at the *COM-B Model*. What do you remember?

Jamie Blimey. Well, there's *Capability (C)*, *Opportunity (O)*, and *Motivation (M)*. They're all connected and can change *Behaviour (B)*.

Robert Top marks. And we're going to focus on the *M – Motivation*. There are two possible methods you can use to bring about change. The first is *changing the person*. This may involve changing the way they think and feel or changing their habits and routines. It includes much of what we talked about earlier – identity, beliefs, values, and a sense of self. Changing the person will change the way they react to a given situation or the way they shape their own lives.

Jamie What's the second method?

Robert The second is *changing their environment* – this means leaving the person as they are and focusing on their situation. You do this by changing the physical and social world they inhabit. This can range from changing the size of plates in a school cafeteria to how we design our cities.

Jamie So, there's a lot of scope.

Robert Imagine a smoker who is interested in stopping smoking. She goes to visit her GP about a persistent cough, but, while she's there, she sees a poster about a local stop-smoking group which has high success rates. Just seeing this poster might trigger her to join the group and have a go at stopping. Nothing much has changed in the way she *thinks* or *feels* about smoking, but the poster has triggered her to *act*.

Jamie I see. She hasn't changed – she was interested in stopping and still is, but the poster just helped turn her desires into action.

Robert Exactly. Contrast that with a situation where the GP tries to persuade someone that they should stop smoking. The person doesn't really want to, so the GP will need to work on changing how that person thinks and feels.

Jamie That's going back to the first method: changing the person. I'm assuming that's a harder battle.

Robert Not always.

Jamie How would you approach that?

Robert Well, let's say we're dealing with certain kinds of behaviour such as stopping smoking, cutting down on drinking, exercising more – behaviours that require a conscious decision to change and, almost always, a battle to avoid going back to old ways. In these situations, my colleague Andy McEwen – who runs a national training programme for stop-smoking advisors – and I came up with a model called *The 3Ts: Tension, Triggers, and Treatment.*

Jamie Catchy name. How does it work?

Robert Let's return to our smoker. She is already experiencing *tension* about her smoking. In other words, she's uncomfortable about her smoking. That doesn't mean she's going to do anything about it herself. But when she sees the poster, it takes the feeling she has and turns it into action. It *triggers* her to actually do something.

Jamie So, triggers can be tiny things?

Robert Absolutely. They can be something as small as having run out of cigarettes and not wanting to go to the shop because it's raining outside. That's the final straw and the person says, 'You know what? I'm done with this!'

Jamie What other kinds of triggers are there?

Robert It depends on what behaviour you're trying to change. If you want to give up drinking, it might be waking up with a hangover, a chance remark from a friend, a TV documentary... the list is endless.

Jamie Triggers seem to be things that tip people over the edge into finally changing something that had been bothering them.

Robert Right. Although it's not always conscious. Sometimes the tension is buried beneath the surface. To me, it's like an earthquake – tension builds up, but no one can see it. Then, suddenly, apparently out of nowhere, energy is released, and the ground starts shaking. Some people refer to a trigger as an 'epiphany' or 'Road to Damascus' moment.

Jamie So, tension is really *'motivational tension'* – feeling uncomfortable about the current situation and a sense that you should do something about it. Triggers are events that turn this into action. What do you mean by 'treatment'?

Robert I'm using the term 'treatment' very loosely – I was looking for a word that starts with a T! Treatment is anything that helps *sustain* the behaviour change. In the case of stopping smoking, it can be taking a pill such as Champix (a stop-smoking drug), counselling, or even a book such as *The SmokeFree Formula* written by the two of us!

Jamie And these things help?

Robert They do. But it is important to recognise that everyone is different, and people must feel comfortable with whatever is being proposed. In *The SmokeFree Formula*, you will recall that we use the phrase, 'I guide: you decide'.

Jamie I remember discussing the importance of respecting the reader's right to choose their own path.

Robert I think the message of agency and empowerment is vital with any kind of support one is offering to sustain behaviour change.

Jamie But the treatment has to suit the person.

Robert Yes. Otherwise, any work you've done on tension and triggers will be wasted. You need all *The 3Ts* working together. And if one of them fails, you won't change the behaviour.

Tension

CREATE OR BUILD ON DESIRE FOR CHANGE E.G. EDUCATE, PERSUADE, REWARD, PUNISH, MODEL

⬇

Triggers

USE SOCIAL OR OTHER CUES TO TRIGGER ACTION E.G. PROMPT, REMIND, SHOW

⬇

Treatment

PROVIDE SUPPORT TO MAINTAIN CHANGE E.G. ENCOURAGE, TRAIN, FACILITATE, PROBLEM SOLVE

KEY POINTS

- There are two possible ways to affect someone's motivation: *change the person* or *change their environment*.

- Changing the person involves changing the way they think and feel or changing their habits and routines.

- Changing the environment means changing the physical and social world they inhabit.

- We can change behaviour using *The 3Ts: Tension, Triggers, and Treatment*.

- Tension (or 'motivational tension') is where a person feels internally conflicted about a situation and feels they should do something about it.

- Triggers are events that turn tension into action.

- Treatment is anything that helps to *sustain* the behaviour change.

9. Creating Tension: Persuasion

Jamie Tell me more about tension in motivation. If someone is already dissatisfied with their current behaviour, a trigger can tip them into action. But what if there's no tension in the first place?

Robert If there really is none, and it's not just that it's under the surface, we have to create it. And one very important tool is *persuasion*.

Jamie I see. What exactly is persuasion?

Robert Persuasion can be defined in many ways, but I like to think of it as the act of trying to get someone to *feel* differently about something so that they *act* differently. Very often we do this by trying to get them to *think* differently – but not always.

Jamie We're in 'changing the person' territory. And feeling is important here?

Robert It's crucial. It isn't enough for someone to say, 'Yes, I accept that drinking too much causes liver cancer, so gin can be dangerous,' if they don't feel anything about it.

Jamie A cerebral understanding alone doesn't help.

Robert Correct. And this is very common if you look at the rhetoric in politics or in public health. So much of it is people saying, 'If only we could educate the public about the costs of unhealthy behaviour, then they would do the right thing'.

Jamie Doesn't that sometimes work?

Robert Only if it makes them *feel* differently.

Jamie Okay, so, how do you go about persuading someone?

Robert The most common method of persuasion involves creating *cognitive dissonance* and then shaping the way people reduce it.

Jamie What's cognitive dissonance?

Robert Cognitive dissonance is an uncomfortable feeling we have when we hold beliefs which appear to conflict with each other. Being uncomfortable, we then feel a need to do something about it. For example, if I'm told that my best friend, Bob, whom I believe to be a good person, has committed a murder – that would cause me to feel cognitive dissonance.

Jamie So, the two opposing thoughts create tension – how can Bob be a good person *and* a murderer?

Robert Right. Now, there's nothing illogical about this. Good people can do terrible things, but it's a *psychological* inconsistency. It makes me feel uncomfortable.

Jamie Ah, back to the feeling again. How would your brain cope with the conflict?

Robert There are several different ways. I can refuse to believe the new information. I could say to myself, 'He couldn't have done it'.

Jamie You hear that all the time in the news when they interview a family member of someone who is on trial for a crime.

Robert Or, I could say, 'I was wrong about him'. But that would mean re-evaluating everything I think and feel about my friend. And that may mean I have to doubt my judgement, which would cause even more cognitive dissonance and discomfort.

Jamie How does the brain choose which path to go down?

Robert It follows the path of least resistance – like a lightning bolt. And, like a lightning bolt, the path can seem random because tiny things can change it. The subtlest things might lead the brain to take one route over another.

Jamie How does this fit in with persuasion?

Robert We can use persuasion to create tension by highlighting a contradiction in someone's belief system. So, if I'm trying to persuade someone to have a go at stopping smoking, one tactic I could use is to bring one of their beliefs to the forefront of their minds. Let's say they believe they're a good person, but they also think that smoking is their choice, and they have a right to make that choice. I might then say, 'You have people around you who love you and depend on you. They don't want to see you get sick and die. If you get sick and die, that will hurt them. How do you feel about that?'

Jamie That's a tough line to take!

Robert I may soften it a bit depending on the person. But I want them to think, 'How can I, as a good person, hurt the people I love?' and use that tension to guide them towards having a go at stopping smoking.

Jamie You're deliberately making them uncomfortable. But what if they refuse to believe that getting sick and dying will harm their loved ones? Or if they refuse to believe they'll get sick at all?

Robert Good question. They might even say to themselves, 'I don't smoke *that* much'.

Jamie In that instance, they've changed their belief from 'I'm a smoker' to 'I don't smoke *that* much' which might be more compatible with their sense of themselves as a 'good person'.

Robert It might make them feel better – but it won't lead to the behaviour change we want. Ideally, in this situation, we'd be trying to use the tension created by cognitive dissonance to persuade them towards trying to stop smoking and to offer it as the *best* way to resolve the dissonance in their belief system.

Jamie So, in persuasion, we try to bring together conflicting beliefs that a person would find difficult to ignore or dismiss. Then we offer them a path towards resolving that dissonance.

Robert Yes. I'm raising the tension then presenting a way to reduce it.

Jamie That makes me think of Marc Antony's speech to the crowd in *Julius Caesar* – the 'Friends, Romans, countrymen' one. The point he keeps coming back to is that Brutus is an honourable man, and yet he has done this terrible thing. He rouses the crowd against Brutus who, only moments before, had been cheering him.

Robert That's a clever example of the rhetorical use of cognitive dissonance. And this is an important point because if he had said that Brutus was not an honourable man, the crowd would think, 'You would say that, wouldn't you?' Instead, Marc Antony aligns himself with the crowd by saying that Brutus is an honourable man, and yet he's a murderer – so, now we have a shared problem.

Jamie 'Now we have a shared problem'. I like that. And, because they have something in common, this means that the crowd is more likely to have sympathy with him. Any public speaker knows that building rapport with your audience at the beginning of a speech is absolutely crucial. And Marc Anthony makes himself seem trustworthy here.

Robert It's called establishing *'source credibility'*.

Jamie So, going back to cognitive dissonance – a person could refuse to believe one part of the information or alter one of their beliefs to lessen the dissonance. Can they do anything else?

Robert They could suppress one of their beliefs. So, if someone brings it up in conversation, they'd just say: 'I don't want to think about it'.

Jamie Ah. Now, is *suppression* different from *repression*?

Robert Yes. Repression is a psychoanalytic concept in which things we feel uncomfortable about are put into our *subconscious*. So, they might still influence us in dreams or in slips of the tongue. Suppression is simply not thinking about something.

Jamie With suppression, you're putting the uncomfortable idea at the back of the drawer. Whereas, with repression, your conscious mind denies that there even is a drawer?

Robert Something like that. So, sometimes persuasion is just keeping something on the agenda – bringing it out of the drawer. That's the role of a lot of public health mass media campaigns: just keep it on the agenda.

Jamie But does that really work?

Robert It certainly does. There is plenty of evidence that anti-smoking campaigns increase quitting, even if they do not contain new information.

Jamie The mass media campaign triggers action.

Robert Right – by affecting motivation. And even if it doesn't, it still keeps the tension going.

Jamie So, we can refuse to believe one of the conflicting beliefs, or alter or suppress a belief. Anything else?

Robert We can *add* another belief. Let's go back to my hypothetical friend, Bob, the murderer. How can I reconcile my belief that he's a good person with that of him being a murderer? I can bridge the gap by adding a third belief that he might have had a mental breakdown.

Jamie Which essentially externalises the responsibility for his actions. It means that your friend can still be a good person, and you don't feel quite so uncomfortable about the whole thing.

Robert Yes – just as someone who is unhappily overweight can reconcile themselves with the belief there is nothing they can do about it.

Jamie But the problem is that the belief leads to inaction.

Robert That's the whole point. The brain is seeking to reduce dissonance without the person having to physically *do* anything – the path of least resistance.

Jamie So, persuasion is partly about overcoming people's defences: the beliefs they have built up that stop them feeling bad about behaving in unhelpful ways.

Robert You've got to figure out where the cracks are in their beliefs so that you can open them up. That way, you can disrupt their sense of feeling comfortable.

Jamie And you do that by bringing something new to their attention or putting something they already know in a new way so it creates internal conflict.

Robert Yes. With persuasion, you're trying to arouse cognitive dissonance. Then, given there are lots of ways that people can reduce their dissonance, you want to try and channel people towards beliefs and feelings that are going to lead to the behaviour change you're looking for.

Jamie You're guiding them towards a particular solution.

Robert If a person with an alcohol problem says they can't stop because they're addicted, a doctor might say, 'I understand, but we have effective treatments now that can help people in exactly your situation'. This might resonate with the person in a new way which could potentially trigger a change. It's a bit of an art. And you need to understand that the best approach may be different for different people.

Jamie The offer of effective treatment is essentially undermining the patient's belief that there's nothing they can do about it – taking away that erroneous, comforting belief and re-establishing cognitive dissonance.

Robert Which you can then use to guide them towards behaviour change.

Jamie Is it only public health campaigns that try and create dissonance like this?

Robert Not at all. You see it everywhere. And it's especially common in advertising. The advertiser will try to persuade by creating tension, triggers, and treatment all in one – or at least with repeated exposure to the same advert.

Jamie It makes me think of cosmetic surgery and beauty products. So many adverts for them appeal to our vanity. To take a – uh – totally fictional example: if I saw an advert on the bus promoting hair transplants, it could create tension about me losing my hair. I'd suddenly feel keen to find a way to minimise the tension. But, lucky me, the solution is right there – framed in a very helpful way!

Robert Totally fictional?

Jamie I never ride the bus.

Robert (*laughs*) Well, just seeing that one advert probably won't change you as a person that much. You merely had a disposition to feel a certain way about your appearance. And it made you feel a particular way for a few moments, or a minute or two.

Jamie But those feelings can be surprisingly intense.

Robert Intense enough for you to take action or *plan* to take action. Let's think about your fictitious advert. The problem it seemingly throws up is hair loss. But I think it plays on a whole host of other worries too. If you lose your hair, will you be less attractive? Will other people think less well of you? Will you be treated differently at work? These can be big fears. And the solution – the hair transplant – seems to restore not only your hair but all these other imagined losses too.

Jamie And the solutions in adverts always seem so simple and easy. Get a painless hair transplant, and get the life you really want.

Robert Talk about persuasive! And being presented with an easier solution can be very effective. It can alter our beliefs about how hard changing our behaviour might be. Say you wanted to take an evening acting class but thought the closest one to you was over an hour away. If I mentioned I saw a poster for a new class at the end of your street, there's a much better chance you'd go.

Jamie Because I'd have increased *Capability* and *Opportunity*?

Robert Back to the *COM-B Model*. Very good!

Jamie Can we return to what you said about the intense emotions that trigger behaviour change being short-lived? It makes me think about some of the mindfulness meditation courses I've done where they talk about just watching things rise and fall without reacting to them. You practise observing your thoughts and emotions come and go good-naturedly. And one of the immediate insights that meditation offers is to show just how transitory our experiences can be – although, in the moment, they can be very powerful.

Robert As anybody walking past a patisserie will know.

Jamie It's a kind of stepping back, learning to sit with the tension – to sit with that uncomfortable feeling without immediately trying to minimise it. And by observing the things that push and pull us, we're better able to pick the useful ones to act on.

KEY POINTS

- Persuasion is the act of getting someone to *feel* differently about something so they *act* differently.

- The most common method of persuasion is by creating *cognitive dissonance* and then shaping the way people reduce it.

- Cognitive dissonance is an uncomfortable feeling we have when we hold beliefs which appear to conflict with each other, e.g. 'Bob's my best friend – but Bob's a murderer'.

- Our brains may try to resolve cognitive dissonance by refusing to believe one of the pieces of information, e.g. 'Bob couldn't have murdered anyone'. Or by adding a third belief, e.g. 'Bob must have had a mental breakdown'. We can also resolve cognitive dissonance by simply not thinking about one of the unpleasant beliefs.

- It is possible to trigger someone into action by helping them to realise the desired behaviour is easier to do than they previously thought, e.g. telling someone who wants to get fit that a new gym has just opened up around the corner.

10. Tricks Of Persuasion

Jamie Creating *cognitive dissonance* and then channelling the way it gets reduced is key to *persuasion*. But how do you get people to believe what you're saying and not simply dismiss you?

Robert In an ideal world, we would believe things that have good evidence and arguments for them. The reality is very different, alas. There are numerous tricks of persuasion that people use and it's important to be aware of what they are. One of them is simply repetition. Strange as it may seem, there's lots of evidence that simply repeating a proposition often leads people to accept it. Much of advertising and political propaganda works this way.

Jamie Really?

Robert Yes. Simply repeating a proposition leads people to accept it.

Jamie Didn't you just say that?

Robert Did I? Anyway: simply repeating a proposition leads people to accept it.

Jamie I see what you're doing.

Robert But persuasion is more effective if the same message is repeated by different sources – or *appears* to come from different sources.

Jamie We're more convinced when we hear the same thing from different people.

Robert Yes. You can see this might have an evolutionary advantage for humans. If information is coming from different sources, we're more likely to think it's true. It balances out the biases that might lead to one person saying something.

Jamie That makes sense.

Robert But another important thing to recognise is that humans have a natural tendency to believe what other people say.

Jamie Really? But didn't we say earlier that we reject someone if we don't trust them – if they don't have *'source credibility'*?

Robert Yes. But unless we have a reason to put our defences up, or what someone says immediately arouses a sense of outrage, we will *tend* to believe something we're told.

Jamie I wonder if I'm doing that now!

Robert (*laughs*) I'm saying this with great certainty, and for all you know it could be complete nonsense.

Jamie Uh…

Robert Don't worry. I'm not making it up. Obviously, our tendency to believe puts a lot of power in the hands of people who control the statements we're exposed to.

Jamie Although, people say you can't believe what you read in the press.

Robert People say that, but mostly we *do* believe what we read. The thing is, it would be extremely exhausting to have to question every statement. Our brains can't deal with it. But, as a scientist, I often think the world would be a better place if we started treating all information with suspicion unless we had strong evidence to support it.

Jamie In the era of 'fake news', it might not be a bad idea to be more sceptical.

Robert A follow-on from this is that we are more likely to believe something if it makes a good *story*. We want to believe good stories.

Jamie I'm certainly a sucker for a good story. I once played a concert in Trafalgar Square, and one of my fellow performers told me that nobody knew what material the famous lion sculptures were made from and that this mystery material never eroded. I was so impressed, after the gig I told one of my friends about it. He looked at me oddly and said, 'They're bronze. And they've clearly eroded a bit'. I felt rather silly.

Robert It made a good story.

Jamie Like the ever-punctual Alec Guinness – what a satisfying idea that the great man was never late. So, the more something sounds like a good story, the more we should question it?

Robert Absolutely right. Now, I need to point out something else about persuasion. If we're engaged in trying to change behaviour through persuasion, we have to remember we're not the only player in the arena. There are others who are trying to persuade people of entirely different things. A lot of the art of persuasion is about neutralising the persuasive power of other players.

Jamie You're competing against other stories and persuasive people. So, how do you take them down?

Robert I'm not sure I'd put it like that! But it's good to be on the look-out for the kind of dodgy practices that are commonly used. One of these is to distort an opponent's arguments. You claim they're saying things that they're not – or you present their views in a way that makes them look stupid. An example of this is a process called *belief inoculation*. You present a weakened version of the opposing argument. It's a bit like a polio vaccine in a sugar lump where you're given a dead version of the polio virus. The body then produces antibodies, and when the real thing comes along, your body destroys it.

Jamie You present a weakened version of the argument, and when the person you're trying to persuade hears the real thing, they'll have already discounted it. Is that like the straw man technique?

Robert Yes, the straw man technique is an extreme version of that: totally inventing an argument and pretending your opponent is saying it, which makes it easy to knock down.

Jamie What other tricks do people use?

Robert Another one that is very widely used is to discredit your opponent – either by trashing their motives or their competence. You may try to discredit them entirely so that it doesn't matter what they say, or you may attack their credentials on a particular issue. Again, this plays on destroying their source credibility. In rugby terms, you might call it a high-tackle. You've injured them, so they can't play anymore. They can shout from the side-lines, but they're no longer in the game.

Jamie Is there any time you reckon it's okay to discredit your opponents?

Robert Sometimes: if your opponent genuinely has a vested interest. So, if they're saying something because it's in their own interests to say it. But – and this is absolutely crucial – it must never be a substitute for directly addressing what they're saying. It is never right to argue that just because someone is not a credible source, you can discount what they're saying without evaluating it.

Jamie The magazine *Private Eye* is full of instances where they reveal that a politician is supporting a certain policy because they have shares in a company that will profit from it.

Robert And that should make us very sceptical about what they are saying, but we still have to evaluate it on its own terms.

Jamie When a person makes an argument, sometimes you hear the response, 'You would say that, wouldn't you? You're a liberal/conservative/socialist!'

Robert This is a bit different. You're discounting someone's views because of who they are. In your eyes, their view is explained by their membership of a group, so you feel entitled to discount their opinion. Of course, this is nonsense – but it doesn't stop us doing it.

Jamie It does occur to me that we're telling people all the secrets of how to take advantage of one another!

Robert It's certainly a risk. However, one of the reasons for alerting people to these tricks is that if we're aware of them, we can recognise when others are trying to manipulate us. It empowers us to say, 'I'm not falling for that one!'

Jamie That eases my conscience a bit. So, we've looked at *The 3Ts: Tension, Triggers, and Treatment* and the role of cognitive dissonance in persuasion. We've also recognised that unless something makes us feel bad, we're inclined to believe it. And we've looked at a few tricks of persuasion to get people to believe the things we say. What else?

Robert Another important tool of persuasion is *reciprocity*. With any situation in which you are trying to help someone change, it's important to create a sense of, 'I give you something; you give me something'.

Jamie But in the case of a counselling session, isn't it the counsellor who should do all the giving? After all, aren't they being paid to do that? What does the patient give?

Robert It's not about money. It's more general: I behave positively towards you, so you behave positively towards me.

Jamie The offer of treatment is a friendly and positive gesture that can prompt a positive response?

Robert Right. And it helps to make the patient an active participant in the process. For example, if you go to your GP and they mention there are some great weight-loss courses available, and they ask if you'd be interested – they're making you an offer.

Jamie The GP has shown some generosity. But what if the offer is rejected, and the patient says they don't believe anyone can help people to lose weight?

Robert Well, crucially, the GP *doesn't* say, 'You're being ridiculous!' The GP makes it clear they hear and understand what their patient is saying, so the patient feels respected. Then the GP can try and use a persuasive technique. It might simply be giving some new information or pointing out the evidence. But always remembering it's a dialogue not a monologue.

Jamie This is one of the advances in doctor-patient relations in the last few decades, isn't it? Realising a heavy top-down approach can be counter-productive.

Robert And that's partly down to reciprocity.

Jamie Is there anything else you want to say about persuasion?

Robert Well, it's a massive topic and we have only scratched the surface here, but I hope I've given a few tips on how to do it well and how to recognise when someone is trying to manipulate you. In essence, when we're persuading someone of something, we're getting them to *feel* differently about something.

Jamie So, the change has all been internal.

Robert Exactly.

KEY POINTS

- Simply repeating a proposition often leads people to accept it.

- Persuasion is more effective if the same message is repeated by different sources.

- Humans have a natural tendency to believe what other people say.

- We are more likely to believe something if it makes a good story.

- A common persuasive technique is to misrepresent your opponent's argument and then knock it down.

- Another common technique is to disparage your opponent, destroying their credibility.

11. Incentives

Jamie Zooming out from the massive subject that is *persuasion*, what are some of the other motivation tools we can use?

Robert Another key tool is the use of *incentives*.

Jamie Do you mean *rewards*?

Robert Kind of.

Jamie What exactly is an incentive?

Robert An incentive is creating an expectation of a reward for behaviour someone is, or isn't, going to do. Now, of course, you may promise a reward and not give it. However, if you do that, people will soon realise that you're not reliable! So, usually, incentivising someone goes along with actually giving them the reward. But it's worth bearing in mind that it's the *expectation* of a reward that affects behaviour.

Jamie What different kinds of incentives are there?

Robert I like to distinguish three types: *financial*, *personal*, and *moral*.

Jamie Let's start with *financial incentives*. How do they work?

Robert As we've discussed, money plays such a crucial role in our lives. We say that money can't buy you love, but it *can* buy you most other things. If I offer you a million pounds to do a particular task – whatever the task is – the money is a massive incentive. It can be exchanged for a huge variety of things, and that's what makes it valuable.

Jamie So, that relates to extrinsic motivation. What's a *personal incentive*?

Robert It can be anything else that makes you feel good: doing a job well, winning praise, taking part in activities you enjoy – like going to the cinema.

Jamie That's connected to intrinsic motivation, got it. And what are *moral incentives*?

Robert That's about being incentivised to do things that fit with your values. It's important to realise, however, that our financial and personal incentives typically set the boundaries within which we pursue our moral incentives. In other words, if it doesn't cost us anything financially or personally, we're perfectly happy to do things that fit with our morals. But as soon as it starts to genuinely cost us something, then moral incentives tend to take a back seat.

Jamie I remember being a student and noticing that if I had a bit more money, I'd buy organic milk from the supermarket. But if I felt a bit pressed for cash, then I bought ordinary milk. And it struck me every time that morals often cost money. Some people can *afford* to be more moral than others.

Robert And now you're experiencing cognitive dissonance because you didn't behave in accordance with your moral values! So, what did you do?

Jamie I ended up saying to myself, 'At least I buy organic milk when I can afford it'. And sometimes, on a bad day: 'Organic milk is a bit of a rip off, anyway! Don't think about it!'

Robert Very often, cognitive dissonance causes our moral values to come into line with our financial and personal incentives. We come to believe that the things that make us happy and well-off are morally right. But I don't want to give the impression that moral incentives always take a back seat. There are people who make huge sacrifices for others, putting their moral incentives above personal and financial ones. Where do you think their behaviour comes from?

Jamie Erm...

Robert A strong *identity* as someone who holds those values. Some people, some of the time, override personal and financial incentives. But for most of us, most of the time, that's simply not how we operate. By and large, if you want people to act in a 'moral' way, then you need to structure things so that this doesn't conflict with other incentives.

Jamie Why did you do air quotes when you said 'moral'?

Robert Because, obviously, there are many different ideas about what is morally right. Which leads me onto an important point. When you're trying to change someone's behaviour, you can generate financial and personal incentives, but many of the values that drive moral incentives are internalised by the time we're adults.

Jamie They're deeply ingrained.

Robert Those morals will have been assimilated during a process we call 'socialisation'. This is the process that takes place during childhood and adolescence when we internalise social rules and norms and determine our place in society.

Jamie So, if I'm trying to persuade somebody right here and now, I'm going to struggle to change their basic value system.

Robert Indeed. But values obviously do change as the cultural climate shifts. Most people in countries such as the UK now consider drink-driving immoral. But in the 1950s and 1960s, it was quite normal and accepted.

Jamie Even later. The 70s song 'In the Summertime' by Mungo Jerry, has the line: 'Have a drink, have a drive'!

Robert I hope that was tongue-in-cheek! From a practical viewpoint, if you're trying to get someone to change their behaviour, you're unlikely to persuade them to change their morality in the short term.

Jamie But ... Now, let's see if I've got this right ... You might be able to create cognitive dissonance by getting them to realise that some of their existing morals conflict with other beliefs that they hold?

Robert Spot on! And then we're back in the realm of persuasion.

Jamie How do you make incentives work so that people don't come to rely on them? Or have them backfire like with the GPs who were being paid to encourage people to stop smoking?

Robert Unless you are going to be able to keep the incentive going, you need to think of it as a starter motor. For example, if you want someone to go to a weight-loss clinic, you can incentivise them to go in the first place. But once they've started going, you want the behaviour to be rewarding in and of itself to keep the person attending.

Jamie Is that why trial sessions are sometimes given free? They act as a starter motor incentive to get people to go in the first place?

Robert Afterwards, people may be willing to pay for the sessions because it's become a personal incentive for them to attend. Incentive structures can be very powerful.

Jamie Doesn't that sort of take away the idea of individual agency?

Robert Not really. To give an example: addiction doesn't make you do things – it makes you *need* to do things. Which is subtly, but crucially, different.

Jamie You're saying incentives don't take away our agency, rather they make us *want* the things that are being incentivised? My brain is starting to hurt...

Robert Yes. That's why the lines between intrinsic and extrinsic motivation are often so blurry. But, I would say that a sense of agency is critical to all of us. Without it, we'd be in trouble.

Jamie There are a few interesting studies suggesting that when people stop believing in free will, they start to act in more anti-social and unpleasant ways. But isn't it somehow immoral to direct someone's free will where *you* want it to go?

Robert Well, that's what everyone is doing all the time. We are all active agents influencing each other. It sounds a bit like sophistry because you're getting someone to do something different from what they otherwise would have done, but you're not *making* them do it.

Jamie And that's the 'playing-with-fire' aspect. We've been talking about these tools in the context of how to achieve our goals individually and collectively, but they can be used for good or for bad.

Robert You sometimes hear people complain about the 'nanny state'. And they're basically saying people should be free to choose what they want to do, and the state shouldn't get involved. But if they really believed that, then they wouldn't believe in corporate advertising either because it is obviously manipulating people's desires. The big difference is that in a functioning democracy, you can vote out a government that is trying to influence you in ways you're not happy with – you can't vote out corporations.

Jamie I guess we all have our own individual incentives, and very often they don't align.

Robert It's a complicated business!

KEY POINTS

- An incentive is creating an expectation of a reward for behaviour someone is, or isn't, going to do.

- There are three types of incentives: financial, personal, and moral.

- A financial incentive is an offer of money. A personal incentive is anything that you genuinely enjoy. A moral incentive is about doing the 'right thing' based on your core values.

- Our financial and personal incentives usually set the boundaries within which we pursue our moral incentives.

- Unless you are going to be able to keep an incentive going, you need to think of it as a starter motor, e.g. a free gym session which leads to the person signing up for an annual membership.

12. Coercion & Punishment

Jamie We've talked about *incentives*, which are about creating positive expectations. Now, tell me a bit about *coercion* and *punishment*. How and when should we use these?

Robert There are a few key things to remember. The first rule, which we touched on earlier, is: *don't use punishment unless you absolutely have to*. There's a moral reason for this but also a very practical one: it motivates people to avoid the punishment and the source of the punishment, rather than change the behaviour you're punishing.

Jamie Instead of being motivated to stop behaving badly, you just work harder not to get caught!

Robert Exactly. Another problem with punishing is that it also models bad behaviour. Because human beings are very imitative, the use of punishment can lead to more punishment, and society can rapidly descend into a destructive cycle. A quote attributed to Gandhi sums it up: 'An eye for an eye will leave everyone blind'.

Jamie So, people who have been punished also tend to punish. What's the solution?

Robert A guiding principle in motivation is: *if you want someone to do something, you should try to get them to want to do it.*

Jamie And if you can't do that?

Robert Then you may need to coerce them, and that's where punishment does comes in. Either scaring people about the consequences of behaving badly or of not behaving well. And in order to do that you need to know what people fear. What they like and don't like.

Jamie This is starting to sound like a manual for a medieval torturer! What do you mean by 'you may need to coerce them'?

Robert Whereas incentives create an expectation of *reward*, coercion creates an expectation of mental or physical discomfort if the desired behaviour isn't performed. So, when you were kids, we used to threaten to turn the car around and not go to the restaurant if you and your brothers kept on squabbling.

Jamie I remember that happened quite a lot...

Robert It's not ideal, obviously. But threats, large and small, play a big role in controlling our behaviour. A lot of people would behave very badly if they weren't afraid of being punished for it. The criminal justice system is based largely on that.

Jamie And does it work?

Robert Well, there's a lot of assumptions in the criminal justice system that people fear the punishment they'll receive if they commit a crime. But in many cases people don't. When you're dealing with people who have serious behaviour control problems and repeatedly end up in prison, a major part of the reason is that they don't fear the punishment.

Jamie They're not afraid of the consequences?

Robert Exactly. The punishment – and this is a common theme – may make the punisher feel better, but don't expect it to deter people from committing crimes.

Jamie I guess there's a natural tendency in people behaving badly to think that everything is going to turn out okay. They're focussing on things going to plan and getting what they want.

Robert And when you talk to people who engage in reckless acts that endanger their own or other people's lives, you say, 'Why? Don't you realise the risk you're taking?' But, for some people, it isn't a risk because they think it'll be all right. So, it's important to get through this self-protective cocoon.

Jamie Essentially denial.

Robert Right. And, interestingly, when the bad thing does happen to people who behave destructively, they usually attribute it to something else – bad luck, etc. It wasn't because of something they did.

Jamie I suppose the thinking is, 'I've behaved like this hundreds of times before and gotten away with it. So, the fault must lie with someone else'. But didn't you say earlier that punishment can be very effective?

Robert In the right circumstances. But people who repeatedly get into trouble with the law do so because the normal process of socialisation hasn't worked well for them in the past. And there's little reason to think the process is going to work any better now.

Jamie In other words: the people who we most want to punish are often the ones least likely to learn from punishment.

Robert You got it.

Jamie Presumably you'll need a different tool.

Robert The best way is to create an environment that doesn't foster unwanted behaviour. But if you have to do it through shaping them as people, you may have to turn to reward. That doesn't necessarily mean giving away money, or sweets, or things like that. It might just be getting them to feel positively about themselves – usually as someone who has a new *identity* as a person who has *reformed*. This works well when you have rehabilitation programmes in which the person develops an identity as someone who helps other people. For example, in drug addiction, there are programmes in which people who previously had addiction problems can develop new identities by helping other people to get over their addictions.

Jamie And this becomes a personal incentive, creating a sense of agency, satisfaction, and self-worth.

Robert Exactly.

Jamie But what if that doesn't work? Say in the case of a reoffending criminal?

Robert Sometimes the best thing you can do is reduce someone's opportunity to commit crimes. A lot of anti-social behaviour is opportunistic and driven by the moment. Someone spills a drink on someone else in a pub, one thing leads to another, and someone gets seriously injured, or worse. The criminal hasn't gone into the bar thinking, 'I'm going to hurt someone today'. So, you need to change their environment.

Jamie And sometimes, of course, that can mean putting someone in prison.

Robert It can. Although, it's worth noting that a lot of people in prison are not particularly anti-social and don't have this difficulty learning through punishment. Their life has taken a particular direction, and, if things had been different, they could be out in society living a happy and fulfilled life. But, unfortunately, there are other people in prison who are too dangerous to live with the rest of society.

Jamie We've talked a bit about this, but what's the best way to use punishment?

Robert The most effective way to punish is to signal very clearly what behaviour will lead to punishment and what won't. In other words: the punishment is completely avoidable if you behave in the desired way.

Jamie I bet they've tested this on rats...

Robert You know what? They have! There have been studies with rats looking at what's known as *'signalled avoidance'*. In the experiment, a rat is placed in a small cage, a little light comes on and, shortly after, an electric shock is delivered through steel rods in the floor.

Jamie Oh dear!

Robert *But* if the rat presses a lever, it can avoid getting the electric shock. In that situation, the rat learns pretty quickly. As soon as the light comes on, it wanders over and presses the lever – quite relaxed.

Jamie Doesn't it experience fear?

Robert Maybe a little. It's learned it needs to press the lever and it can avoid the punishment. That's why it's called 'signalled avoidance'.

Jamie That makes sense.

Robert But there's another kind of punishment, which is extremely counterproductive and damaging called *'non-signalled avoidance'*. Brace yourself because this is unpleasant. In this experiment, there is still a shock. There's also still a lever that would help the rat prevent the shock, but, this time, there's no signal. Technically the rat could press the lever every minute or so and avoid the shock, but it doesn't. It never learns to press the lever. It just sits in the corner of the cage cowering.

Jamie What a horrible experiment.

Robert Indeed. But let's transpose this to a more recognisable scenario. If you're a parent bringing up children, you should set very clear contingencies, so the child knows what behaviour will lead to punishment. But if the child is punished unpredictably – in other words, the punishment is not signalled – then this leads to a disrupted socialisation process.

Jamie You mean the child gets punished when they haven't done anything wrong?

Robert Exactly. For example, if the parent is just in a bad mood and snaps at the child. Of course, that's going to happen occasionally. But if the contingencies aren't set, this kind of punishment leads to neurosis. It creates a high state of anxiety all the time which then becomes deeply embedded in the child. And when the child grows up, they find it harder to learn from punishment even when it is signalled. You get what's called *'learned helplessness'* which is when the brain has worked out – not necessarily consciously – that it doesn't matter what you do, you're going to get punished.

Jamie You feel like you're damned if you do, damned if you don't. Because, to the child, the punishments have felt cruel and random.

Robert And even if it isn't random – like we said, it might be caused by the parent being in a bad mood, or whatever – it *feels* random to the child because the punishment is originating from the parent. The punishment is not based on a plan to socialise the child.

Jamie So, a child needs to be told that if they steal a pack of sweets, they will be punished – perhaps by having their pocket money confiscated.

Robert Yes. Although, obviously, you can't signal everything. Part of the process of socialisation is setting up those contingencies so the rules become firmly embedded in the child's psychology. Sometimes, the child behaves badly in an unexpected way, and they don't realise it's bad. In that case, the important thing is to make clear to the child what they've done and why they're being punished.

Jamie Okay. Let me see if I've got this right: The rules of punishment are (1) Don't punish unless you have to (2) Clearly signal what behaviour will be punished and what won't.

Robert And, timewise, try to carry out the punishment as close to the behaviour that you're punishing as possible.

Jamie Won't the person being punished come to really dislike the punisher? How do you stop your kids from hating you?!

Robert You've got to build in some way of counteracting the side-effects of punishment. You try and use warmth and love while you're engaging with the child, and make it clear that you're punishing the *behaviour* not the child. Obviously, as we've been talking about it we've used a shorthand, saying, 'If you punish the child'. But, it's important that the child knows the difference. So, they're not a *bad child*. The underlying message is: 'I love you, but you mustn't behave in this way, or your behaviour will be punished'.

Jamie Whenever we talk about punishment, it always makes me think about a time when kids – and I think this happened to you – used to be caned at school. It seems horrific to us now. But I also think politically in terms of liberal and conservative. Very broadly speaking – and I know there are many times this isn't true – liberals seem keener on reward and conservatives on punishment.

Robert It's an interesting point. I think you're right that people have their preferences of how to achieve a certain behaviour change. Usually, it's in reference to their own experience of being socialised. Some people who were caned at school didn't like it at the time but did find it 'character building' – I wouldn't put myself in that category, though. Many others hated it and found it destructive. And those preferences will emerge when they're discussing how to achieve a certain behaviour-change goal.

Jamie I see. But those preferences may well be unhelpful.

Robert Yes. Once you've decided on the goal you want to achieve, you need to find the *best* way to achieve it. But there are people who prefer to punish or reward, irrespective of their effectiveness – and that's a problem.

Jamie Isn't that just an argument for the ends justifying the means?

Robert Fair point. You can't use any means because means create other ends. Let's take a hypothetical example: even if it were the case that you could get more effective behaviour by putting a gun to someone's head, that wouldn't necessarily make it the best thing to do because it would have knock-on consequences. You have to think about the bigger picture which is one of the reasons why, generally speaking, reward is better than punishment.

Jamie So, punishment in the narrow sense can, in some circumstances, be more effective, but it may have unfortunate side-effects.

Robert Correct.

Jamie I've seen that a lot on social media, where people have a huge propensity to punish in order to try and achieve their goal – which may be a very laudable goal – but the punishment itself causes all kinds of problems. And maybe it's worth it, but maybe it isn't.

Robert It's useful to consider whether there are better alternatives because most of us, when we feel angry or threatened, are inclined towards punishment. But, remember, it usually isn't the best solution.

KEY POINTS

- Coercion creates an expectation of mental or physical discomfort if someone does, or doesn't do, a particular behaviour.

- The people who we most want to punish are often the ones least likely to learn from punishment.

- The most effective way to use punishment is to signal clearly and consistently which behaviours will lead to punishment and which won't.

- Make it clear that you're punishing the *behaviour* not the person.

13. Conclusion: Wrapping Up

Jamie We've come to the end of our discussions on motivation! Let's see if we can round the book off in a satisfying way for our readers.

Robert Good idea.

Jamie Let's take an example and put it to the test.

Robert All right. Here's one: there's a child that's crying and causing a scene in public. Based on the previous chapters, what should the parent or carer do?

Jamie Number one: don't punish unless absolutely necessary.

Robert Correct. Which doesn't mean that the parent won't need to punish the child, but it shouldn't be the first port of call. And don't punish to make yourself feel better – punish if you are sure it is needed to achieve your goal.

Jamie Okay. What next?

Robert First, let's be clear that, in this scenario, the child isn't crying because there's a legitimate problem – they aren't hurt or in pain. If they were, obviously, that would need to be addressed immediately. The next rule is: don't reward the crying with attention or the object of the child's desire. I know it's hard – it's designed to be. The child is using punishment to get you to do what they want! But you can give a reward, such as praise or a cuddle, when the child stops.

Jamie Won't that just encourage them to have a tantrum so they can get a reward?

Robert It might. But you can make the *incentive* part of a wider structure in which they are rewarded for behaving well *without* having a tantrum beforehand. And, over time, good behaviour will move from being extrinsically motivated to intrinsically motivated.

Jamie This was where you use an external reward, including praise, to get someone to start behaving in the way you want, and then in many cases the behaviour itself becomes rewarding.

Robert That's it. Although, of course, there are many situations where you need to keep giving people the external reward, such as when you employ them. Most people wouldn't go to work if they weren't being paid to, even though work provides many more benefits than simply financial ones.

Jamie 'Starter motor' incentives are things like free trial sessions, free samples, etc.

Robert Exactly. And in the case of the child, the incentive may start out as a sweet or extra time on the iPad for behaving well. Then, a personal incentive can slowly transform into a moral one. The child starts to take pride in being well-behaved.

Jamie It gives me a warm glow just thinking about it.

Robert I should say! But remember that the child crying is also an example of behaviour that you may not be able to stop every time. Which is important because, without meaning to state the obvious, there are many things in life we can't change, and there's no point pretending we can! Sometimes you have to choose between two bad options and just pick the least bad.

Jamie Let's imagine that the child has already behaved badly. In other words, you clearly signalled that it was wrong for them to throw Plasticine in your face, but they did it anyway.

Robert In that scenario, you need to emphasise that you're punishing their *behaviour* and not them. If they behave in that way again, they will be punished. If they don't, they can avoid the punishment.

Jamie Essentially reiterating what behaviour will be punished and what won't.

Robert Sometimes it takes time for children, and adults, to learn.

Jamie But now let's imagine your child doesn't respond to punishment at all, should you just keep punishing them anyway?

Robert (*laughs*) I know you're being ironic, but that's what a lot of parents actually do. The obvious answer is that you need to do what works, and, in this case, it's likely to involve rewarding the child for good behaviour – no matter how small. It's counter-intuitive, but sometimes it's the *least bad* option.

Jamie Okay. I'm sure there are plenty of books out there with specific advice about how to deal with crying children, so we'll leave that one there!

Robert Yes, and good luck with that. I'm glad all my children are grown up!

Jamie I don't have quite so many tantrums ... Okay, so at the beginning, we defined motivation as something that energises and directs behaviour.

Robert Right. That was part of the *COM-B Model*. *Capability (C)*, and *Opportunity (O)* set the stage for how we might act. And *Motivation (M)* decides our actual *Behaviour (B)*.

Jamie And I seem to remember that motivation was about doing things and *not* doing things. We discussed poor Phineas P. Gage, who had a rod blast through his brain. It damaged his frontal lobes and he found himself, temporarily at least, unable to function socially.

Robert Yes. Very often, we're trying to stop harmful behaviours as much as promote good ones.

Jamie Now, you take quite a holistic approach to motivation and behaviour in general. One of your big gripes is scientists and psychologists who only focus on one narrow perspective and ignore the others.

Robert That's right. We have to recognise that we can change people's environment and 'nudge' them towards the right behaviour, but we also need to acknowledge the importance of changing people's beliefs, or their biological drives, etc. It's really important to look at a problem from a number of angles in order to generate a wide variety of solutions which you can then select from.

Jamie You also said that we need to challenge our habitual ways of acting and thinking.

Robert Absolutely, whilst acknowledging that it is inevitable – or at least highly likely – that we will revert at some point to our bad old habits. Once you acknowledge that, you can factor it into your plan. If you're on a diet, for example, it's very possible you might binge on junk food one evening, but that's no reason to totally abandon the diet.

Jamie It seems obvious when you put it like that, but that's not how a lot of us act.

Robert It's easy to slip-up and then give up completely. The important thing is to recognise that tendency and take steps to get back on the wagon, so to speak.

Jamie And this is all related to *self-control* which, in turn, is related to *identity*.

Robert And we have to remember that identities are inherently unstable, but a strong *sense* of identity is very important. As you say, it's the basis for self-control.

Jamie Although, now I'm wondering if a strong sense of identity as someone who *can't* overcome an addiction, for example, might be a bad thing.

Robert Yes. Identities can be maladaptive as well as adaptive. But remember that they *can* be changed.

Jamie And when we're trying to change someone's motivation, we can either change them as a person or change their environment.

Robert Yes. And when it comes to changing behaviours that need people to make a conscious effort, you can use *The 3Ts: Tension, Triggers, and Treatment*. To take a quick example: you may be uncomfortable about being unfit – this is motivational *tension*. One day, you see an advert for a new gym in your area, and this might *trigger* you to join it. Then, at the weekend, you have an induction session with a trainer which is the start of your *treatment*. Obviously, I'm using the word *treatment* in a very broad sense.

Jamie And it's possible to create tension in someone by arousing *cognitive dissonance*.

Robert Right. You can create cognitive dissonance by creating or highlighting conflicting beliefs. So, for example, if you were trying to persuade someone who is a workaholic to spend less time working and more time with their family, you may draw their attention to the fact that, although they like to consider themselves 'a good parent', their behaviour isn't in line with this belief.

Jamie It's about creating discomfort then trying to channel that discomfort into a particular action.

Robert There are many ways in which we try to reduce cognitive dissonance when it crops up. We can suppress one of our conflicting beliefs. In other words, we just don't think about it. That's why simply having a conversation can sometimes help bring an issue to the surface, and then it can be dealt with. Another way people deal with two conflicting beliefs is to add a third belief. So, in the case of our 'good parent', they might add the belief: 'I need to work this hard or we won't have any money. I'm doing this for the sake of my family'.

Jamie Which is basically them saying, 'There's nothing I can do about my behaviour'.

Robert Indeed. And that's easier than rearranging one's work schedule to make more time. Our brains will invent any excuse to maintain the status quo.

Jamie What were the persuasive tricks you mentioned?

Robert Simply repeating a proposition often leads people to accept it.

Jamie The power of repetition.

Robert Especially if the information comes from different sources or seems to come from different sources. And, the truth is, we have a natural tendency to believe what other people say.

Jamie Unless we doubt their intentions.

Robert Well remembered. Another tactic is to bring a sense of reciprocity to the exchange: I'm giving you something, therefore you give me something.

Jamie And that doesn't necessarily have to be a financial exchange. As a doctor, you may be offering goodwill, and the patient can respond by working hard to stay with the programme.

Robert The key thing about *persuasion* is that you're trying to get someone to think and feel differently about a situation, without having actually changed anything in the outside world. It's all in the mind.

Jamie Okay, phew, we've made it to the finish line! Are there any final words of wisdom you want to pass onto our readers?

Robert I suppose I'd suggest there are many areas of our lives where an understanding of motivation can really make a difference. Try some of the tools we've laid out in this book – see what works and what doesn't. Don't stick rigidly to strategies that aren't working: be flexible. Be your own experimenter. Understanding motivation can transform your life and the lives of everyone you come into contact with. Good luck out there!

Glossary

Balancing Input: Environmental influences that keep our perceptions, emotions, and beliefs from spiralling out of control. Our brains evolved to be unstable so that they can learn and adapt quickly but at the cost of needing constant external reference points, e.g. in 'sensory deprivation' experiments, people who are immersed in a tank of water at body temperature with no light or sound may start to hallucinate.

Behaviour: In humans, physical activity involving our voluntary muscles, co-ordinated by our central nervous system.

Belief: Any proposition that we hold to be true with some degree of confidence. This includes specific beliefs such as, 'It will probably rain tomorrow' and more general ones such as, 'Smoking causes lung cancer'. It also includes evaluations such as, 'Failing my exams will be disastrous' and 'Reducing our carbon footprint is important for our survival as a species'.

Belief Inoculation: Presenting a weakened version of an opposing argument so that your target audience develops antibodies to it and discounts it when the real version comes along.

Blame: Assigning moral responsibility for something that is judged to be bad.

Coercion: Creating an expectation of a negative outcome if someone does, or does not do, something.

Cognitive Dissonance: A feeling of discomfort associated with holding two or more conflicting beliefs.

COM-B Model: Capability, Opportunity, Motivation, and Behaviour. For any behaviour to occur, the person must have the capability, opportunity, and motivation to do it. The components of the model interact with each other.

Evaluation: A belief representing or implying a degree of good or bad, right or wrong, usefulness or harmfulness.

Goal: An imagined scenario that someone wants, needs, or intends to achieve.

Identity: The disposition to have particular thoughts, feelings, and images about ourselves.

Incentive: A valued outcome expected to arise from doing, or not doing, something. There are three types of incentive: financial, personal and moral. Financial incentives involve money, property or services. Personal incentives relate to pleasure, and physical or mental discomfort. Moral incentives involve satisfaction from acting in accordance with moral values.

Learned Helplessness: A condition that affects people and animals in which unpredictable punishment has taught them not to try to avoid punishment.

Motivation: Brain processes that energise and direct behaviour, including plans, evaluations, desires, habits, and instincts.

Need: A feeling of attraction to an imagined future scenario associated with anticipation of relief from, or avoidance of, mental or physical discomfort.

Persuasion: Using communication to change how people feel about things.

Praise: Expressing a positive moral judgement for something judged to be good.

Punish: Causing something negative to happen to someone because of something they have, or have not, done.

Reciprocity: A tendency of people to respond in kind to each other's behaviour. Kindness tends to breed kindness, and hatred breeds hatred. Showing respect for the other person's position can make it more likely that they will listen to and accept your arguments.

Resolve: The motivational strength to enact a plan in competition with other motivations, e.g. by inhibiting an impulse.

Response: Starting, stopping, or modifying a behaviour.

Reward (noun): A positive event: one that causes pleasure or satisfaction, or meets a subjective need.

Reward (verb): Causing something positive to happen to someone because of something they have, or have not, done.

Secondary Reinforcer: A stimulus that comes to act as a positive or negative reinforcer as a result of being associated with a reward or punishment, e.g. the feeling of smoke being drawn into the mouth and lungs comes to reinforce the act of smoking because it is immediately followed by a 'nicotine hit' which is rewarding.

Self-control: The moment-to-moment control of behaviour by plans and evaluations, e.g. resisting an iced-ring donut when on a diet.

Signalled Avoidance: A process in which an animal learns to avoid a punishment by responding to a signal predicting punishment if action is not taken, e.g. a rat will easily learn to press a lever when a light comes on to prevent it getting an electric shock. It is distinguished from 'non-signalled avoidance' in which there is no warning about the impending punishment, in which case animals find it very hard to learn how to avoid punishment and end up being anxious.

Source Credibility: A characteristic of a message source, whether it be a newspaper, business, government, or person, that leads to people trusting it and believing what it says.

The 3Ts: Tension, Triggers, and Treatment: An approach to promoting lasting behaviour change. Create motivational *tension* so that the person is dissatisfied with their current behaviour. Provide *triggers* to translate that *tension* into action, e.g. using prompts and cues. Provide *treatment*, which is broadly defined as anything that helps to sustain the new behaviour, whether it be teaching coping responses, maintaining resolve, or finding alternatives that meet the underlying need.

The Unstable Mind: A model of the way the human brain operates which recognises that it evolved to be unstable and extremely responsive to environmental inputs. This has the advantage of enabling very rapid learning and adaptation but has the disadvantage that it needs constant 'balancing input' to prevent it spiralling out of control, e.g. when alone with our thoughts at night, we can start to create unnecessary worries by wild imaginings.

Urge: The subjective experience of an impulse to perform a specific behaviour.

Values: Widely applicable beliefs about what is good or bad, e.g. lying is wrong. Values can be given a relative priority, e.g. murder is worse than lying.

Want: A feeling of attraction to an imagined future scenario associated with anticipated pleasure or satisfaction.

Acknowledgements

We are deeply indebted to Aliyah Kim Keshani for editing *Energise*. We would also like to thank the students of University College London's Summer Schools and MSc in Behaviour Change for their invaluable comments on the draft versions of the text.

About The Authors

Robert West is Professor of Psychology at University College London and an Associate of UCL's *Centre for Behaviour Change*. He is Editor-in-Chief of the specialist scientific journal *Addiction*, and he has published more than 800 scholarly works including books on behaviour change, addiction, and smoking.

Jamie West is a writer, performer, and musician. He holds a BA in English from UCL and an MA in Creative Writing from Birkbeck University. He performs as a solo musician and with his band, *The Banished Poets*. For more information, visit: www.jamiewest.net.